# Wisdom Wishes

## How to turn anxiety into a gift that will connect your family

*Thank you for being part of my journey*

*warmest wishes*

*Sinéad*

*xxx*

**ORLA KELLY** PUBLISHING

## Sinéad Flanagan

# Advance Praise

This lovely book is filled with love and dedication and is a beautiful follow-on from your classes. It is a wonderful support to parents who need it to help them see they have the power. It really will bring so much calm and comfort to families.

**Marneta Viegas, Founder of Relax Kids**

This book is fantastic. I will be recommending it to parents and the students on my courses.

**Louise Shanagher. Children's therapist, mindfulness teacher and Psychology lecturer**

Wisdom Wishes has been a blessing sent to us. What a fantastic book. I felt as if the book had been written for me and hit many nerves in a great way. As a mammy with a daughter who had been very anxious and so worried since COVID-19, this book really has made me see how to ease and help soothe her. The way in which it's written is so easy to grasp and understand. It's unique. I have been using it since, and it opened my eyes and mind to turn the anxiety around in such a positive way. We now have a happy house and a happy child. Every mammy needs this book.

**Jenny, Westmeath**

*The beginning of freedom is the realization that
you are not "The Thinker."*

The moment you start watching the thinker, a higher level of consciousness becomes activated. You begin to realise that there is a vast realm of intelligence beyond the thought, that thought is only a tiny aspect of that intelligence. You also realize that all things that truly matter – beauty, love, creativity, joy, inner peace – arise from beyond the mind.

You begin to awaken.

*Practicing The Power of Now* by Eckhart Tolle

*This book is dedicated to all the parents out there who strive everyday to do their best with the knowledge and ability that they posses in that moment.*

# About the Author

Sinéad "Neade" Flanagan is a social care practitioner by trade. She obtained her Social Care Honours Degree as a mature student. She started her career as a co-ordinator of a Garda Youth Diversion project. She then started her family and having returned to her role as co-ordinator expecting her second child, she made the decision to give up full time employment to raise her children.

While she enjoyed the role as parent, she did find it challenging to be a full-time parent. She then trained to be a Napro Practitioner to assist couples in their quest to be parents. It allowed her to work her own hours and use her own experience of infertility to benefit others. It was during this period of work that her interest in wellness, nutrition and positive mental health was sparked. She witnessed first-hand the impact clients thought process can have on fertility outcomes. She found the old saying your thoughts create your reality particularly relevant. Sinéad is a country girl at heart and very passionate about prevention being better than cure. She also believes in functional medicine and empowering people to make informed choices. In response to this growing interest, Sinéad discovered the Relax Kids Programme.

Initially she just purchased some of the books to help her children wind down and get a restful sleep. The books were so successful that she made the decision to train herself. This was a turning point for Sinéad. It has changed her life, her connection with the world around her and most importantly her children and extended family.

Sinéad has since gone on to train as a charge up coach, Wise Hippo Birthing Instructor and Riahanni Energy Healer. She is passionate about people, community, equality and equity for all.

Little did Sinéad know how important the Relax Kids training was to become for her little family unit. Anxiety threatened to rob her child of being present. She noticed that her child was in her head processing constantly and Sinéad was devasted. Now when your child is struggling and it's impacting your child, as a mum you want help now, not in months' time as is currently the experience for a lot of people. Sinéad took on the journey of using the Relax Kids seven steps to help her child with Anxiety. Coaching her to manage it herself and teaching all the family how to support her in a way that was empowering for her and promotes self-reliance.

She runs relax Kids programmes in schools both 6-week programmes, one off Anxiety Workshops and family sessions. The one-off Anxiety workshops involve Sinéad working with the children and then facilitating a talk to the parents later that evening. Sinéad also initiated a workshop for parents which involved a nutritionist, occupational therapist and herself.

Sinéad is a mum to 3 children. She is a wife, sister, neighbour and spends half her time on the side of a hurling or football pitch cheering on the two eldest. Her baby has just started big school and dance classes. She lives on one of the only hills in the midlands in Ireland and loves the view of the bog that appears to change throughout the day. She loves the outdoors, cooking, nature especially butterflies, clothes, eating out and movie nights. She is passionate about buying local and sustainable food and products. She meditates regularly and is spiritual by nature. Sinéad's gut instinct guides her life and choices. She is a heart centered person who believes that were all equal regardless of status or title.

# Contents

# Wisdom's Wishes

This book fills in the gap between professional psychologist and granny. So, you're aware your child is struggling, and their behaviour is having a negative impact on themselves, you as their parent, and the family unit. However, it's all small stuff, little battles to get them out the door for school, repetitive arguments about mundane issues, sudden tummy aches, headaches, or refusals to go places that they enjoy. Falling asleep has become this major challenge, and they lay there wide awake until exhaustion gets the better of them or you end up bed-surfing until they give in to exhausted sleep. Sometimes you feel that they have forgotten how to laugh and you're wondering where your little happy bub has gone. It's confusing. Who is this new person and how do I get the old one back? Where do I start looking for help? This book outlines my experiences and responses to anxiety in my child.

I truly hope the following pages will inspire, motivate, and irritate you into thinking. It's not a directional-focused book telling you how to parent. You as the parent, I believe, are the highest authority on your child. You live, breath, and feel all their successes and hurts. You are there on the front line when disaster strikes. Thus, it's in all of our best interests that you navigate your particular parenting journey as your family sees fit and appropriate for you. It is my hope that this book will challenge you to do that in a way that utilises truth, love, compassion, and wisdom as its compass.

I believe that, if we learn to parent from the heart and meet our children's needs, we will naturally evolve into a nation whose children can express their truth. Children who get used to expressing their truth and having it respected and met with compassion and love will evolve naturally into humans who are balanced, centred in themselves, loving, respectful, and empathetic of others and nature. This can only be a good thing for us all as individuals but also for the greater good. We are all born with a spark of light which needs to be nurtured to bring it forward. This light, our truth, our individual creativity is much needed. Imagine a world where we all pulled together and supported each other, a place where we learn to negotiate differences and meet each other halfway. No judgement, just love.

I chose to approach dealing with anxiety in my child from an empowering perspective. I could have used books to manage the feelings and distracted her into feeling better. That just didn't sit right for me. Don't get me wrong, that approach has a place, but just not for me. I feel that we must honour our children with the truth. I felt very driven to demonstrate with my behaviour that I felt confident that she has what it takes to understand, accept, and control her anxiety. The greatest gift we can give our children, I believe, is the knowledge that everything they need is inside them. No matter what happens, no matter what chaos is befalling them, they always have a choice to connect back into themselves, into their own wisdom. Allowing it to guide them to their highest wishes, the holy grail being the discovery of your child's own Wisdom's Wishes.

# Chapter 1

# Anxiety: The Brain–Body Connection

*The Triune Theory* on the brain is, I believe, the simplest and most comprehensive theory on how our brain works. It provides a way of understanding how our brain, body, and emotions interact with each other. It gives us a road map for how things work when we're all calm and chilled and when that anxiety monster strikes. When I was introduced to this information first, I remember thinking, *If only I'd know this when I was a child.* The point of sharing this information is to empower our children to understand their thoughts and emotions so that they can learn to accept, share, and manage their thoughts and emotions in a way that's fun, light-hearted, and feels safe for them.

## The Amygdala (Monkey)

This is our internal alarm centre, which keeps us safe. This part of the brain is very reactive, and whenever we feel under threat and upset, it sends stress hormones (a message) via the vagus nerve to the rest of the body, releasing adrenalin and cortisol, which signals the fight, flight, or freeze response. Imagine that your child is crossing the road and gets distracted for just a moment. They then turn their head, and a truck is approaching at top speed. The monkey part of their brain will shout in their head, *"Stop or you be hurt or killed."* The body responds on high alert, the digestive system slows down, heart rate increases, and all bodily systems are focused on just staying alive. Their body is flooded with stress hormones. Every cell in their body is totally focused on staying alive. That's a good thing when it's short term only. There are times in their lives when they need to be alert, focused, and totally switched on. The killer here is, however, that for a child with anxiety, they are having the same all-over body reaction just going into school or taking a test on a Friday morning. In addition, science tells us that it takes the body anything between twenty and thirty minutes to return to normal, calm functionality after a short-term stress episode. In the short term, like crossing the road, the monkey is our friend and keeps us alive and safe. We don't need to focus our energy on digestion in that moment. Once we get across safely, our monkey relaxes, and normal functionality returns. However, this is not the case for the children who are anxious about everyday occurrences, like school or speaking in class. Instead of an acute, once-off event, it's chronic, prolonged, and negatively impacting the body continuously.

That monkey part of the brain is still perceiving the world as if were in the caveman era. I need to fight, flight, or freeze. It has not developed the ability to understand that the test won't kill you or trying something new is not going to hurt. Essentially this part of the brain is not very bright, but it is complex. It is important to understand that this monkey part of our brain reacts the same to a perceived threat as it would to a real threat, and feeling threatened can mean many things to different people, especially children who are anxious. When your child is in a state of fear or anxiety, they *cannot think* because their monkey brain is totally focused on survival.

Stay still for a moment and think about a time when a person said something negative or dismissive to you. In that moment, you felt hurt and under attack. Your body reacted, the space around you closed in somehow, your heart rate increased, or your palms got a little sweaty. The reaction is different for everyone, but the outcome is the same: nothing comes out your mouth. In that moment, you fail to express yourself because your monkey brain reacts, and you feel under attack and therefore cannot in that moment respond. Moments later, or sometimes hours later, your brain runs through countless scenarios of how you should have or could have responded, but the moment has passed.

## The Hippocampus (Elephant)

This part of the brain stores memories and manages how things make us feel. Sounds lovely and simple right, yes, but very impactful for children. Let me explain. When your child comes home from school, they don't just see the house and think, *Oh look, a set of bricks all put together.* They feel all the connections and memories that the house contains. It's a safety net, a comfort blanket after their day. When they rush in the door and throw the bag down and smell the dinner, that evokes memories of family connections, dinners gobbled down because they were starving, and a place where they feel warm and where it's safe to be themselves.

When they go to school, they don't go into class and see their teacher and think, "*Oh there's a human.*" They know its Miss or Mr. Teacher. Importantly, they also register very quickly that they know what's acceptable and what's not, they know what they can get away with and what they can't get away with. In my experience, the anxious child will also be gifted at taking the emotional temperature and will register instantly whether the teacher is in good form or not.

So, this part of our brain allows us to make associations between places, relationships, objects, sounds, smells, and how they make *us feel*. It stores information for us to dip into when required, for example, for the test on Friday morning in school. It also stores how we feel about these things so, therefore, it helps us to remember we are loved and cared for. We have adults in our lives that meet our needs and places where we feel safe, which are all-important feelings to have, but especially on the days when life feels overwhelming. That smell of your favourite dinner when you open the door after school or a kind look from a teacher can soothe countless hurts. This is particularly important for the anxious child.

## The Prefrontal Cortex PFC (Owl)

This area of our brain is the most evolved since we left the cave. It's the part of our brain that we use to speak, problem solve, create, imagine, and organise ourselves. For children, this area is not fully developed or fully mature until, for girls, they are approximately twenty-five and boys approximately twenty-eight. Some wives argue older but that's a whole other book, LOL.

For children in general, they need lots of support and help from caring, calm, relaxed adults to nourish this area of the brain to allow them to flourish. For me, that means being aligned or attuned to who they are on an internal level. To be able to be creative, problem solve, or do any of the functions of this area of the brain, a child needs to be able to think. This might sound simple, but it's incredibly challenging for any individual, let alone the child with anxiety.

Remember, I mentioned how we've all had the experience of somebody saying something negative or hurtful to us. We feel awful and don't respond in that moment. Hours later we replay the conversation in our minds and have a lot to say for ourselves, some of it colourful. So why can we not speak our mind in that instance, and why is it only after time has elapsed that our truth flows? Science has the answer. For us as humans to be able to access the Pre-Frontal Cortex (owl) and or our Hippocampus (elephant), our Amygdala (monkey) must be calm/relaxed. Therefore, when we are stressed, emotionally upset, or feel threatened, *we cannot think*. Anxious thoughts can literally shut down parts of our brain. Remember I said the monkey part of our brain is functioning like we are still in the caveman era. Any situation can be perceived as being in danger of being eaten or being safe. If I'm in danger, all non-essential functions of the body will be shut down so I can focus my energy on staying alive. I notice these children in class because they have a look, that pale, washed-out, dark circles under their eyes, not rested, not relaxed, they are in their head in class and not responding to what's asked of them, but rather reacting to it. In family sessions time and time again, when explored, parents will report that their child never looks restful in bed. They move constantly in their sleep and when checked while sleeping rarely look what I describe as zoned-out, arms outstretched, face relaxed of expression, quiet and still.

Our anxious children are, therefore, potentially experiencing this high-alert stressed state constantly. Their monkey brain is literally on alert always, albeit a low level but constant alert, denying them access to their thinking owl part of their brains and aligning them into a thought pattern that leaves them feeling disassociated with their main caregivers. Remember the pathways to their comfort zone via the elephant brain, i.e., memories and feelings, are also blocked by the monkey. These children are running a mental marathon constantly that they are often too young, stressed, immature, and exhausted to express.

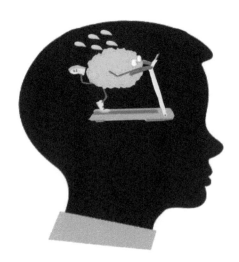

Imagine that you are an anxious child and try to put yourself into their thought pattern for a moment. They feel like they have to have it all figured out and are, in my experience, constantly watchful. Their monkey brain is in charge, driving their behaviour and reactive responses to their environment. In my family sessions and my own personal experience, anxious but functioning children will zone in or focus on one parent. For the anxious child, this parent's presence is their comfort blanket to a degree. On some level, the monkey brain will relax somewhat if that parent, usually Mum, is present. All hell may break loose if Mum announces that she is going out or, God forbid, staying away. For the anxious child, this elicits a feeling of utter panic. Remember, the monkey does not know the difference between real and imagined danger. Panic and all sorts of challenging behaviour can occur, such as blood, snot, and tears. Some children will attempt to contain the fear through control tactics. These coping behaviours will be expressed through requests for details and questions like *how long will you be gone?, who will be there?, will you be drinking?, who's driving?,* and the list goes on and on. This is all in a vain attempt to calm their monkey's incessant anxiety for the child.

Having read this piece on the brain, can you now understand that your lovely bundle of joy has not suddenly turned into somebody you don't recognise and possibly don't like very much? Can you now understand that their behaviour is a cry for help, as they don't have the knowledge, understanding, or language to express how they are thinking and feeling?

Thoughts create our behaviour, so understanding how the thought process works is the first tool in our kit to tackle that monkey brain and ensure that it works for us and does not prevent our children from living expressive, fun-filled, full, calm, and creative lives.

*Anxiety is just a thought!* Yes, just a thought; however, for the anxious child, that thought gets stuck like a car on a roundabout with no clear exit. The more they sit with the thought and it gains momentum on each circle of the roundabout, the more power it gains, the greater the impact on the child's body via stress hormones, thus the greater the feelings of fear they will experience. Remember, for them, this feeling of fear is very real and very overwhelming. Imagine that feelings are bubbles of energy in the body and that anxiety creates energy bubbles that expand and move constantly the more you think and dwell on them. Eventually they take over the body until it becomes too much, and the child has no choice but to discharge the energy.

Now I, as an adult, can recognise this feeling and can discharge this energy in a healthy way through movement like dancing, a run, or a walk and talk session with my bestie. Children have not learned this skill yet and thus it gets expressed as aggression, argumentative verbal communication, and the child even creating flashpoints, for example, asking for a different hat just as you're rushing out the door. This is a little like crying when we're emotional; painful to go through, but we feel better afterwards. The anxious child needs to discharge, or they will spend their day unable to be present, too emotionally supercharged to respond positively to anything.

Let me sum it up with an example I use in workshops with children. Imagine it's Friday morning and your class test is happening. I place — actually I usually throw — three puppets (monkey, elephant, owl) in three corners of the room. It's fun to see children react to an adult throwing objects. I request children walk over and stand by the puppet which represents the area of the brain they will use to complete the test, requesting that they don't confer and remember that there is no right and wrong answer. I'm just interested in what they think. Usually it's a split response, with the majority going to the owl, a few going to the elephant, and maybe one or two heading to the monkey.

Nobody is completely right in their response or wrong. You need the focus and alertness of the monkey to ensure you show up and are present for the test. No point in being there, daydreaming, looking out the window thinking about Friday night's pizza. Then you need the processing ability of the owl brain to read the questions or listen to the questions and understand what is being asked of you. Lastly, you need elephant brain to be able to remember what you learned that week. So, actually, you need to be balanced in the centre of yourself, getting the best from all elements of your brain. It's like life, really: it's good to be balanced, calm, and responsive to all of the experiences that life has to offer so you can learn how to respond and get the best from yourself and have your needs met.

What I want you to do with this information is share it with your child. I use puppets in class and family sessions to illustrate my point. Once you have taught them each part of the brain and what it is responsible for, move on to the diagram of the brain and thoughts. Walk them through the fact that anxiety is just a thought. It's not good or bad, it's just a thought, and the following pages will provide you with practical actions that you and your child can use to soothe that monkey thought and help restore calm so that your child can think clearly and restore full functionality in the body.

Ideally, I'd like you to go forward from this point asking your child questions about how they are feeling. We can all fall into the trap of asking: what's wrong with you? There is never anything wrong; it's more about uncovering what they are feeling. If that feels too intense for your child, then focus on questions that move it into the third person. *How is that monkey making you feel? Is he being cheeky this morning?* Okay, let's try to help him calm down. The following pages will outline action-based tools you can use to help your child learn how to distinguish their anxious monkey thoughts from what's real. It's by no means an exhaustive list, but that's a good thing. Get creative, run around the kitchen after your child if that will make them laugh, challenge the monkey to a Tik Tok dance and see how that works. Remember, you're the expert on your child, so you'll figure out what works best and when for them and you. You got this, Mama!

*This chapter is dedicated to the memory of Ana Arravoe, a beacon of light who inspired many, including me, with her ability to love freely both herself and all lucky enough to share in her presence.*

# Chapter 2

# Anxiety in Motion

When I work with class groups, run workshops, and facilitate family sessions, I request that participants help me out a little. The aim of this exercise is to consolidate the learning and appeal to anybody whose learning style is visual. I use open language and also request that they say the answers aloud, thus helping to ensure that they are engaged and actively participating. I think we have all been in workshops where the speaker drones on and our mind goes to the beach. If we want our children to learn to manage their monkey brain, then they need to be truly clear on the brain-body connection and how they interact. It's amazing to watch the impact of this exercise on children and adults. With a short sequence of questions, you will see realisation dawn and the light bulb go off that all these feelings, all the anxiety they experience, the overwhelm, the tummy ache, the loose stool, the sweaty palms…they all start in the same place and they start small. If we can teach them to lean into it instead of resisting it, we can all learn to manage its power and negative impact on the health and happiness of our families.

**The Owl Brain (Pre-Frontal Cortex)**
- Most evolved
- Responsible for thinking, creating, organising, problem solving, imagination, and language

**The Amygdala (Monkey)**
- Internal alarm centre
- Very reactive
- Fight, Flight, Freeze
- Focused on survival

**The Hippocampus (Elephant)**
- Stores memories and feelings
- Creates connections
- Links relationships, objects, sounds, smells, places with feelings

I think you should familiarise yourself with this exercise and complete it with your family. Get a piece of paper and some pens and complete it together. It might be a great idea if Mum and Dad run through it together first. Start with a blank page. Simply ask your child to draw a large circle for the brain. Then pop another shape inside the circle to represent the monkey brain. Ask your children to remind you what the monkey brain is responsible for. Get them to list its impact on the body and its ability to shut down the other parts of the brain. Ask the question, *Do we need to listen to the monkey? Yes, we do, as it keeps us safe, but we also need to learn when to tell him that he's okay.* I go back to the example we used in an earlier chapter of having to complete a test on a Friday morning. We need to listen to the monkey part of our brain so that we are focused and alert and ready to answer the questions. We can't be sitting in class gazing out the window, wondering what's for dinner this evening. Furthermore, if the monkey is too loud in our heads and taking over, then we will be too stressed to pay attention.

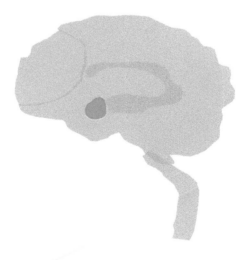

Next explore the elephant brain. Again, draw a shape inside the original circle to represent the elephant brain. Request that together you explore what that part of the brain is responsible for, which is storing memories and processing how we feel about things. Ask your children to close their eyes for a moment and try to remember a good experience they had recently or a holiday they shared with you. Request that they stay with the memory, focusing on how they feel when they are remembering. It may take some children a little while to get it. Ask questions like, *Can you remember doing something on holiday that you had never done before,* or *Did you eat something delicious? Can you focus your elephant brain and feel it again?*

It's fabulous to watch their expression change while their eyes are closed. Reaffirm for them the functions of the elephant brain are to help us store our memories and process how they make us feel, helping us to understand that we are loved and cared for. Skip back also to the Friday morning test example. Remind them that they need this area of the brain to access what they learned in class and while completing homework.

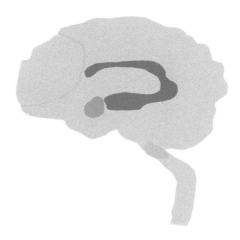

The wise old owl part of our brain, request that they draw a circle within the original shape. Run through all the functions of this part of our mind. Our owl allows us to speak, problem solve, create, imagine, and organise ourselves. I would especially focus on two key take-homes here. Firstly, the fact that this part of the brain allows them to speak and express their needs. Secondly, the fact that it's not fully developed until they are in their twenties. For a child, that is forever away. I want them to get from this that they don't have to have it all figured out yet, but they have lots of potential for growth. Remember, the brain can form new pathways and highlights to them that, even if they are currently finding something challenging, they have the ability to retrain their mind to work for them. Chat about the Friday morning test again and how they need the owl brain to process what is being asked of them.

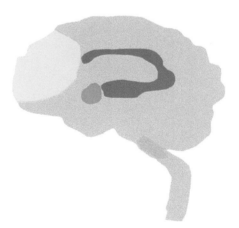

Participating in the test on Friday morning requires them to get the best from themselves by balancing the input from the three areas of the brain, as we covered in an earlier chapter. *So why does the monkey get out of balance and block our access to the other areas, leaving us stuck, so to*

*speak? What happens to start him off, what tips the balance in the wrong direction?*

Ask these questions aloud, and you may hear responses that are situational, for example, "*He's afraid of the teacher's response,*" or "*He thinks I won't remember anything.*" All potentially correct, but *what starts him off? Why does he become active and take over your brain?* I have at this point facilitated many of these sessions and very rarely do I get the answer I am seeking. Guess what? *Its just a thought.* Use a pen to pop a single spot on the centre of the circle depicting the monkey part of the brain. It's just a single thought. See diagram below:

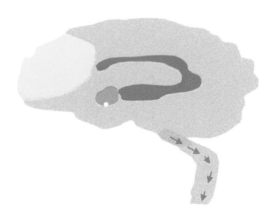

How can a single thought have such a potentially negative impact on our brain function and our body? Remind them about the vagus nerve and its messages to the rest of our body. One thought is not that powerful, but with anxiety, what happens is we get stuck on that thought and allow it to repeat in our minds like a car on a roundabout failing to exit. The more we think the thought, the more powerful it becomes and the stronger the impact on our body.

Draw the increase in size of the original dot in the monkey brain with your child. Tell them to imagine that they are repeating the negative thoughts and thus they are growing and getting more powerful. Eventually you are getting the thought dot to a point that it gets so big that it takes over all of the brain circle, controlling their actions and how they feel, leaving them unable to access their elephant and owl brain. See below for an example.

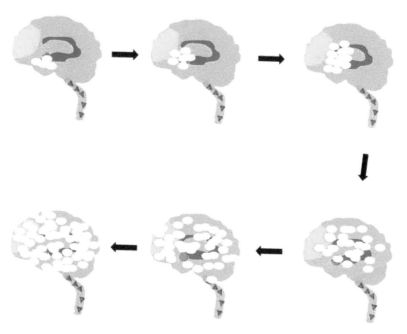

If the monkey brain is activated by a single thought, and is at its weakest in the beginning, then ask your children, *When do you think we should start to work on managing it?* Help them understand that resisting the monkey and attempting to avoid him will only allow him to gain more power. All the activities we have learned or are going to learn (depending on when you choose to cover this with your children) will help us manage our monkey thoughts so that they don't overwhelm us. We can with practice kick the monkey's butt, stunt his growth, and learn to be present, calm, and responsive to life.

# Chapter 3

# Anchoring Techniques

*"Yesterday is history, Tomorrow is a mystery, Today is a gift, and that is why it's called*
***The Present."***

**Bill Keane**

## The Now Clock

How many times have we heard, but "what if"? What if this, that, or the other happens? For a small combination of two words, "what if?" sure packs a powerful punch. The little cheeky monkey called anxiety can get hundreds and hundreds of possibilities out of "what if?" It can induce a panicked response in both children and adults alike. It literally steals your child's focus from the present.

In the beginning of our journey with anxiety, I really struggled with the words to respond succinctly and age appropriately. It also at times felt like a solid brick wall to break through for my child. It can be so difficult for children to grasp the notion that, yes, all their what ifs could potentially happen, but also all their potential positive what ifs could also happen. Anxiety can carve out a map of how the journey will unfold, and no amount of signalling or indications from us as parents are going to be enough for them to change how they are thinking and thus feeling. Anxiety lives in the future or the past but never the now. It's creating scenarios of what might be or how a person was thinking or what they meant when they behaved a certain way or said something.

Thankfully, at a Relax Kids training we were introduced to the Now Clock and, OMG, it was a game changer. The Now Clock is simply a picture of a clock as seen below. I used to keep one in my kitchen stuck onto the cupboard wall and another in the car. When your child is having a moment, ask them, "*Right now are you safe?*", "*Is anything going to hurt you right now?*", "*Is that person here that said something hurtful to you?*" It may take a little repetition and coaxing to begin with, but they'll soon cotton on. Try your best to keep the question as light-hearted as possible. I've been known to run around the house asking, "*Is that person hiding in my home?*" while throwing cushions all over the place. Combining movement and laughter for your child is always a winner. Once you get the positive response "(yes, okay, right now I'm with my family, I'm okay)", then ask them to use the Now Clock as an anchor to calm their monkey brain and help them to understand that they're okay.

First, request that your child exhale, helping them to release anxious tension that has built up in their body. Now ask your child to place their finger on the one, request that they take a breath in to the count of four through their nose, hold to the count of four, and exhale to the count of eight out their mouth like they are blowing out candles. Repeat the same pattern as mentioned before, in through the nose and out through the mouth. Ask the question again: "*How you are feeling in your body right now?*", "*Is your monkey calming down?*" Then gauge the response, the physical facial expression, body language, and the verbal response. If you're not satisfied that they are yet calm, then repeat, asking your child to move to number two and take two breaths. Repeat these steps until you see the change you desire happen. It appears that you are not doing much, but remember the monkey blocks the access to the elephant and owl. Simply requesting your child to place their finger on number one and breathe is a knockout combo for that cheeky monkey. Your child is now utilising other areas of the brain, helping to kick that monkey's butt!

To begin with, this process took a time investment of twenty minutes or more. Anxiety seems to create pathways in the brain that become unconscious and entrenched. It felt like I was asking her to walk up hill while her feet were stuck in mud. The anxiety response was automatic for her, similar to how I choose the same route to drive to the supermarket or school drop-off. Science now tells us that the brain is capable of creating new pathways and that it's possible to learn to bypass old responses and create new ones. This information kept me focused and determined. Yes, it's challenging for her, and, yes, at times it felt intense to hold up the mirror to a then-six-year-old and ask her to look inwards, to face her thoughts head on, and then explore how they were making her feel. Hell, I know a lot of adults who don't have the courage to do that! The flip side of that, however, is that she's learning at a young age how to connect into herself, understand herself and her emotions. I totally believe that our emotions are our guiding light. They are the signal from our higher self, our intuition that something is off with us. When we learn to listen to these signals, we are much more likely to express and explore our needs calmly and in a timely manner. Children who learn to express their needs and get used to having them heard, respected, and met will, I believe, grow into adults that are more empathic of others, Mother Nature, and the world in general. Surely that would be a good thing for all of us. We are all born with a spark of light inside us, and this light which is our innate creativity is much needed in the world. Our children are not units of productivity but rather units of creativity. Teaching them at a young age to feel empowered to understand themselves is potentially immensely powerful. It brings to mind a poem by Shel Silverstein that I recite at the end of all my meditations in class, which sums it up beautifully:

> There is a voice inside of you, that whispers all day long, I know
> that this is right for me, I feel that this is wrong. No teacher,
> preacher, parent, friend, or wise man can decide,
> What's right for you.
>
> *Just listen to the voice that speaks inside.*
> **Shel Silverstein**

As soon as your child signals verbally or through their body language that they are feeling better, follow with a positive affirmation. Affirmations are simply just saying something positive about yourself in the present tense, such as, "*I am amazing, beautiful, bright.*" We all feel a little silly saying these types of things for the first time, but you and your child will get over that quickly enough. You can make this fun and light-hearted. We channelled our inner haka! We stomped around the kitchen pulling funny faces and said aloud that "*I am fabulous*" or something similar. Combining movement and a thought pattern is a knockout punch for our monkey brain. On occasion, most children will resist saying something positive about themselves; it's natural to be hesitant. Again, get creative, request your child use a very posh English accent to say their affirmation or try saying "*I am calm*" like a lion's roar. There are literally hundreds of combinations you can have great fun with. Once your child has communicated to you that they have restored calm in their bodies, remind them of all the skills they can use to stay calm and centred and get on with your day. We have already learned about focused breaths, affirmations, and movement. Have some fun and do your best to keep it light-hearted and impersonal. It's not your child, it's the monkey driving their behaviour and reactions.

## The Senses Game

Managing the build-up to an event or the school test on Friday morning or whatever sparks anxiety in your child can be incredibly challenging and time-consuming for the family. It's not easy to see your child's monkey induce panic and thus sometimes extreme behaviour when you're on a timeline to get to school or attend an event. Hands up, armed with the knowledge that the monkey brain shuts down the owl part of our children's brain, I decided that getting anywhere on time was no longer a priority for me. What is the point of getting your child there on time if their little body is too stressed to take anything in? I decided there and then that supporting my child to kick the monkey's butt was my top priority. Looking back now, I realise how cool that was for her. I was communicating with my attention on her that she was my priority. I was also indirectly communicating to her that I believed that she had what it took to kick his butt, that it was achievable for her. To me, that's love in its real sense.

The senses game involves you asking your child to focus on their five senses. Ask them to pick one sense, for example, touch, and describe the texture of something they can touch or remember the feel of. It sounds really simple, but it requires your child to think and thus divert their attention away from the monkey thoughts, reducing their power. Next ask them to pick another sense and this time pick two things they can see, then three things they can remember the taste of, four things they can hear, and lastly smell. It's simple, not complicated, and can be great fun. One of the times we played this game, my child exposed their underarm, saying, *"Hey, smell this!"*

Hopefully, you get the idea that you are distracting their focus and encouraging their creativity, all areas of the brain which are unrelated to anxiety, allowing their body moments of recovery. In the beginning, this might require a time investment from you, but I promise over time it will lessen. For my family, we usually ended up playing this game on the car journey to school.

Use your imagination here. There are tons of other games you can play in the car, such as word association games, taking the first letter of a number plate and thinking of a girl's or boy's name. Spotto is another favourite in our house, thanks to the Aussie Flanagan's. You all agree on a colour of car that you watch out for. It's usually yellow for us, as they are uncommon. The first person to spot one and shout "*Spotto*" gets a point, and the first person to five points wins. As I said earlier, play around, have some fun, find what works for your little unit, and run with that. Enjoy.

# Chapter 4

# Relax Kids Magic in Motion

Relax Kids was set up by Marneta Viegas in the UK in 2001. Marneta was originally a children's entertainer and noticed over the course of thirteen years that children's attention was decreasing during her shows. They were becoming more hyperactive and less able to concentrate.

Marneta wanted to help children find their 'calm' and, having practised meditation since she was twelve, she believed that this would be the answer to helping children maintain focus and concentration. However, at that time, meditation for children was almost unheard of and she had to find a way to make it acceptable to adults/parents. To make meditation for children exciting and more accepted by adults, she transformed many popular children's stories (e.g., Jack and the Beanstalk and Sleeping Beauty, etc.) into creative and imaginative visualisations. Also, having trained in performing arts, Marneta used some of the techniques she had picked up (e.g., breathing from singing, drama games, etc.) and devised a unique seven-step programme that would help children become more calm and relaxed, helping them to focus and concentrate better.

Relax Kids Helps Children:
- Learn valuable relaxation tools
- Develop good mental health
- Build self-confidence and self-esteem
- Build emotional resilience
- Self-regulate feelings and emotions
- Develop focus and concentration
- Become more imaginative and creative
- Manage anger, anxiety, and stress
- Provide them with a toolkit to help manage difficult emotions and life situations
- Increase brainpower and feel happier!

I strongly suggest that you take your child to a Relax Kids class. If there are no classes close by, then have a look at the Relax Kids website, as there are plenty of coaches offering online solutions. Alternatively, Relax Kids has an extensive list of free downloadable resources plus books that you can purchase.

Without consciously understanding that I was doing it, I started to use the seven steps to orientate our day. The Relax Kids Seven Steps are, I believe, a perfect roadmap for health. This is especially true for the anxious child. I believe family life needs to be fluid, otherwise it can be stressful. Each day I strived to move, play, stretch, breathe, touch, affirm, and relax with my children. I meditate regularly, and my kids use guided Relax Kids tracks to help them relax and meditate in their own way. Here's why it is a good idea and how it can help you and your family's daily experiences. I've included some examples of how I incorporated this into our daily lives.

## MOVE

Movement encourages development of core physical skills, improves coordination, boosts energy, circulation, and a healthier immune system whilst helping release endorphins When I felt that my child was dealing with an anxious thought in the morning (I'd notice facial expressions or that she was distant), I'd call it. It would go something like this: *"Hey, honey, I think that cheeky monkey is active this morning...am I right?"* She'd nod in agreement, usually relieved that I had called it. *"Do you want to tell me how you're feeling or distract him?"* Then we'd either have "The Chat" or distraction would be used, as mentioned earlier. Similarly, if your child is expressing their anxiety through tummy aches or feeling sick, call it and break it down with them. Together then decide which response is best this morning: "The Chat" or movement. Movement can be a bike ride around the house or a dance around the kitchen while brushing their teeth. Hop up and down the stairs like a bunny. The list is endless, so do whatever works for you and the kids and enjoy. This is especially powerful if completed before school, as it wakes up the sensory system after sleep. Additionally, anxious children can get lost in their thoughts, so imaginative movement games are a powerful yet simple way to address that imbalance.

## PLAY

Play encourages and promotes social skills and awareness. Helping to build children's confidence, social interaction, and communication skills. They further develop focus and concentration. Literally anything can be turned into a game. Putting away the socks in our house is great fun. We roll up each pair and place them in separate baskets for each child. They stand at the end of the hall or on their bed and I get to peg them at them while they try to dodge them or catch them.

## STRETCH

Stretching exercises help release physical tension, develop motor skills, body awareness, balance, and flexibility. For younger children, this can be combined with play, for example, let's stretch tall like a giraffe, let's walk like a gorilla, bent over and swinging our arms. Let's walk on all fours down the hall like a cat. Focused stretches are fantastic at encouraging body awareness, which will helps your child connect with how he or she is feeling in their body.

## FEEL

Positive touch boosts the immune system, calms the nervous system, aids the production of oxytocin and endorphins, and lowers stress levels in children. Each morning in our house is anchored with positive touch. We can all get lost in the momentum of moving forward, getting on with our daily lives. Touch is super important for children. I have learned over time to interpret their touch. I can now instinctively understand by how their body relaxes into mine if they are upset or tired or still have one foot in dream land. Nowhere feels quite as safe as Mum or Dad's arms. You can't spoil a child with love and hugs, so use it often. Sometimes if I feel my child is getting overwhelmed and is unable to express her truth in that moment, I simply open my arms to her. When it's accepted, it's magic, but do not take it personally and react when its rejected. It can take us all a little bit of practice to surrender.

## BREATHE

Breath exercises help calm the nervous system, and children feel the immediate effect. Breathing exercises also improve concentration and focus. This is perhaps one of the most powerful tools in your tool kit. Breathing is the first and last thing we do on this planet, and its power is not to be underestimated. Conscious, focused breathing activates the vagus nerve and instantly reverses the stress signals from the monkey brain. It has the power to unplug that cheeky monkey and power up the owl so your child can think again and make a choice, bypassing reactive responses and supporting a calm, measured response. We have covered the calming four, four, eight breath earlier. Another favourite of mine is the lion empowering breath. Place your hand on your belly, breathe in through the nose for a count of four, belly should expand with diaphragmatic breathing, hold breath for a count of four. Lastly, stick tongue fully out of the mouth, then expel all the air, making a lion roar sound. This should not hurt your throat. Encourage your child to make the noise, expelling the air rather than roaring. Do it yourself. Yep, you'll feel silly, but you'll also feel great and powerful.

## BELIEVE

Positive affirmations are simply saying something positive about yourself in the present tense. *"I am,"* followed by a positive word, for example, fun, happy, loved. Affirmation exercises are invaluable for developing the holistic and creative input for every child. Benefits include increased patience, focus, concentration, listening skills, and improved communication skills, a sense of caring, confidence, and self-esteem. Affirmations help children create positive beliefs and so promote positive behaviour. They also help release endorphins into the system, which improves health and a happy outlook. Affirmations are of enormous value in any learning process/developmental process because they help us to fix an idea very securely. If we do this first, as a prerequisite to learning, then the mind is open/ready to accept new ideas, to strengthen familiar concepts, and to release its full potential in connecting these ideas to make sense of the world from a more positive and insightful perspective.

Homework tantrum, anybody? *"I can't do this, the teacher did not explain what we had to do properly, I'm tired, I can't do maths or Irish. I hate the teacher, you, school, and the world."*

Yep, we have all been there, and the energy of the outburst can be so intense. If you manage to catch it in time before it develops into a full-blown outburst, request that your child stop thinking negatively and use a positive affirmation instead. If you think you can or you think you can't, either way you will always be right. Let's kick the monkey's butt and approach this differently. Request the child repeat with you, *"I can do this, I will focus on the task, take my time, and get it completed. I can do this!"*

Here are more examples of positive affirmations:

- I am okay

- I am enough

- I am unique

- I choose thoughts that make me feel good about myself

- I love the fact that I am different and unique

- I love and respect myself

- I feel good about myself

- I believe in myself

- I feel confident

- I am confident

## RELAX

Visualisation helps release physical and mental tension, lower blood pressure, increase body awareness, and give children de-stress and self-management tools. Done regularly, these exercises can help relieve fatigue and promote deeper sleep while improving child anxiety.

Improved deep sleep and general relaxation will improve concentration, listening skills, and memory retention whilst expanding the child's imagination and creativity.

It's impossible for the brain to hold a negative and a positive thought at the same time. How cool is that? Visualisations are a fun tool to help the monkey brain relax. With my children, I tend to use visualisations primarily at bedtime. At the beginning of our journey with anxiety, we really struggled with achieving restful sleep. Visualisations were and still are extremely helpful. Once the children are settled and we're at the point of me leaving them alone in their room, I will ask them to see, feel, imagine, or picture in detail something they would love to experience. We're talking in detail imagination here, the sounds, smells, feel of the experience. What they are wearing, who they are with, and what they'd eat while they are there. In the past couple of months, we have played in Croke Park, designed and slept in a camper van. We have visited Disneyland USA and visited Harry Potter Land. We've driven Land Rovers, combine harvesters, and speed boats.

This seemingly simple activity can have a profound positive impact on the quality of the sleep that your child achieves. Sleep is the foundation of all wellness and, for me, was a starting point in my child's recovery. I couldn't ask her to take on her anxiety monkey while she was wrecked tired. More about sleep later.

## Guided Meditations

Relax Kids has a broad range of books and CDs which have turned fairy tales and stories into guided meditations for your child to listen to while settling in for sleep. When we use these CDs/MP3s at bedtime, I would ask the children to listen and try to imagine what was being described as pictures in their head. You can also purchase books and read the meditations to them yourself if they prefer a voice that is familiar to them. It sounds simple, but it can have such a positive impact on the quality of their sleep, and thus health, when they are calm and relaxed while falling asleep.

Insight Timer is an app that I use regularly to assist in the battle to calm anxiety. I love that you can choose meditation duration. If you need ten minutes to organise yourself or attend to another child at bedtime, this app is user friendly. I particularly love Joanne Callan's affirmation recording, It's Beautiful.

Your list of skills to deal with your child's anxiety now include movement, play, stretching, and touch, both self-touch and parent-child touch, breathing exercises, positive affirmations, visualisations, and guided relaxation. All simple, understandable, achievable skills that your child can learn to use to kick that monkey's butt. Practice makes perfect and I cannot overstate the importance of actually doing these things. Use it or lose it is so relevant here. The more you go through these action-based skills and use them, the quicker the response will be. Remember, we mentioned earlier that the brain has the ability to create new pathways and, additionally, the more you use them, the more unconscious the response will become. Basically, in time, you and your child can rewire their response so that their anxiety is less intense and thus less impactful on their body. You will have a healthy, happy, relaxed, centred, empowered child. I can't answer for you, but that is my parenting goal achieved.

The following chapters will explore in more detail elements of the Relax Kids seven steps, plus other techniques I use to benefit my children's management of their anxiety. It's not a chronological, step-by-step, must be followed formula, but more a what fits best in that moment kinda vibe. Trust that you are the expert on what your child needs in that moment and run with what feels right for your family. If it does not hit the mark, no worries…lesson learned. Try something else. You're all learning and evolving, and it's two steps forward and sometimes two steps back. As long as you're together, you'll work it out. Try to remember that all will be well in the end and if it's not well now, it's not yet the end.

# Chapter 5

# Anxiety and Sleep Issues

It's Thursday night after a long, busy week of lunches, school drop-offs, pick-ups, a birthday party and a school meeting, not to mention work, house chores, and food prep. You're tired and looking forward to Friday night chill-out family time and an early night. Life happens and you have a disturbed night's sleep. You drag yourself out of bed Friday morning, complete the usual routine of lunches and drop-offs, but today you have to drive a four-hour round trip. Another driver cuts you off on the motor way and you respond with colourful sign language. It's happened to the best of us; you catch us at the wrong moment and our response is reactive and aggressive.

Once I understood the brain-body connection and its impact on the body, I felt that I couldn't ask my little one to tackle her anxiety monkey while she was feeling so depleted. Remember, that anxiety negatively impacts the functioning of the whole body. Let's look at it this way: quality, consistent sleep is fundamental for a healthy immune system. It regulates hunger, metabolic rate, weight, and even the compassion you have for others. These effects involve our thinking, choices, and emotional states. In practical terms, it's the functioning of our brain. If

I wanted my little bub to feel empowered and centred enough to take on her monkey brain, then I had to give her a fighting chance. Thus, achieving restful sleep was, for me, the logical first step.

No wonder my child looked like she had run a marathon in her sleep. At times it was difficult to find her in the bed. She could be head at the end of the bed, feet on the pillow. Sometimes she was wrapped up like a worm. I rarely observed her looking restful, arms outstretched, lost in dreamland. Therefore, I decided that I needed to start at the beginning again and _retrain_ her brain to sleep. For many years, we thought that the brain stopped creating connections after a certain age. It has now been scientifically proven that the brain can create new pathways or connections. It has an ongoing ability to adapt to different experiences, and this is called neuroplasticity. Our children can learn how to sleep again. We can retrain their brain to get restful, restorative sleep. Not only that, but neuroplasticity is sub-divided into two types, structural and functional. Structural relates to the strength of the connections between neurons(synapses) and functional relates to the permanent changes in neurons due to learning and development. With help and consistency, we could rewire her brain's response to get more restful, restorative sleep. How exciting is that!

Here's how I approached it with my family:

- Decide on an achievable consistent routine and stick to it.

- If possible, alternate who delivers the bedtime routine (Mum, Dad, whoever so your child body receives consistent message regarding the bedtime routine).

- Accept that, to begin with, it may require a time investment.

- Use the Relax Kids seven steps as your anchor, incorporating all seven steps into the bedtime routine in whatever order works for you. For example, let your child have a quick shower every evening as the first bedtime step, then pop some cream on their skin after the shower that contains lavender to promote sleep.

- Gentle exercise is one of the most effective tools to help aid restful sleep. Consider a quick stroll or walk before bed.

- Make sure they are not too hot, as this can often cause restlessness.

- Screens are scientifically proven to interrupt the signals of the brain for up to four hours after use. Try to limit usage to early in the night rather than the hours before bedtime.

- Avoid sugary drinks and food before bed.

- Switching off is a skill that must be learned, and guided meditation can be exceptionally helpful. As previously mentioned, Relax Kids has an extensive library of books, MP3s and free resources you can use. Insight Timer has tons of free meditations which can be extremely helpful also.

- Make a bucket list of activities you would enjoy, for example, a funfair with your friends or special dinner out or attending an event. If your child is struggling to sleep, choose one and try to vividly imagine you are there. We are talking in detail visualisation, the smells, sounds, who is with you, what are you wearing. This moves you into the imagination centre of the brain, which will aid restful sleep

- If your child has gone through the bedtime routine but is still awake an hour later, get them up.

- Repeat the bedtime routine in a mini version.

- Do not allow treats of any description at the time.

- Return to bed and try again.

I hear you thinking, *Oh but I want to sleep in on the weekend or allow my child to stay up late when it's not a school night*. Cool…eventually you'll get to that point, but to begin with, please do consider sticking to a set bedtime and wake-up time. Achieving this helps your child set a pace for their circadian rhythm, which supports sleep quality and overall wellness.

I have recently come across information on an amino acid called 5htp which promotes restful sleep. I suggest that if lack of sleep or lack of restful restorative sleep are challenges for your house, then have a consult with your doctor to discuss if this supplement in the short term might be beneficial.

# Chapter 6

# Cactus Friend Flower Friend

Friendships can become a source of stress for many children very quickly once they start school. I remember thinking when my child was struggling that maybe all children navigate friendship challenges and get this upset about seemingly little disagreements and differences of opinion. They are just meeting loads of new people and working out stuff on her own in the yard, kinda for the first time. They just haven't learned how to not take every perceived slight so personally and not like it's the end of the world. Gradually, however, I noticed with my little bub that it was weighing very heavily on her.

Disagreements are going to happen, possibly even physical fights and emotional bullying. Unless something very unexpected happens, our children are going to be in class or in this school environment with these children for the next eight years. Therefore, we as their parents can't simply make them feel better by saying, "*Oh, that little so and so is just like her mother. Don't mind her; she has no manners and doesn't know how to behave.*" Our child might feel better instantly but then where would we be? Eventually everybody would be some class of so and so and they'd run out of people to connect with.

Our children spend nearly six hours, five days a week in the company of other kids, so writing them all off in a judgemental way was just not going to work and it just wasn't me either. Additionally, how will our children feel about themselves if they make a mistake, lose their temper, and treat somebody badly? Will they then think I'm a little so and so too? My quest to find the words to help my child navigate these little ups and downs began. What I needed was a non-judgemental path of least resistance that fostered forgiveness and kindness because that's the way I wanted my child to respond to themselves if they acted out of character or made a large bo bo.

Luckily, I stumbled across a post by Plant, Love, Grow on Facebook and it captured my imagination. It introduced the concept of cactus friend and flower friend. It was a simple image of a list of positive and negative behaviours to describe how friends should behave. I just loved it and immediately understood that I could use it to help my child navigate this challenge called friendship.

## Cactus friends
### Get too close and you'll get hurt!

They may pretend to be your friend,
but they are not.
They make mistakes and may
pretend to apologize.
They pick on you or others.
They want to control you.
They ask you not to tell others
if they have hurt you.
They don't want you
to have other friends.
They don't let you have a say over things.
They say bad things about you
in front of you.
They say bad things about you
behind your back.
They hurt your feelings on purpose.
They make you feel bad
about the way you look.
They don't care about your opinion.
They like to get you in trouble.
They create stories
about you that are not true.
They make you feel miserable.
You don't feel safe
when they are around.

YOU are allergic
to cactus friends.

## Flower friends
### Everyone blooms together!

They genuinely care
about you as a friend.
They make mistakes
and apologize.
They are respectful of your feelings.
They like you as you are.
They make sure that you are safe.
They understand that sometimes
you want to play with other people.
You can work things out
when issues come up.
They will not tease you
if you tell them to stop.
They will talk to you directly
if there's a problem.
You can discuss together if you
have bruised each other's feelings.
They support you
and encourage you to be yourself.
They respect your opinion
even if it's different.
They like to play and have fun with you.
They tell the truth.
They make you feel good
about yourself.
They want to spend time with you.
You feel safe
with them around.

YOU want to bloom
with other flower friends.

All remarkably simple and straightforward, right? Yes, except how you deliver them and frame them is very important. Life happens, and at times we get it wrong…the best laid plans and all that. As I've mentioned before, people can say and do things that make us feel pretty crappy or self-conscious. This is especially true for little kiddies who are learning to navigate the world both externally and internally. Setting boundaries and finding the balance between letting shit go and taking some learning from an experience can potentially be life changing. The thing is, with kiddies, best friends today can be full-on foes tomorrow and vice versa. You don't want to be falling out with the neighbours constantly. To explain the application of flower friends and cactus friends, I have used an example below. I hope you find it clear, understandable, and that you feel empowered to use it going forward with your own child.

So little Mary and Jonny usually behave like flower friends. They play and have fun and get on well. Then Tuesday after school Mary comes home extremely upset because little Jonny hurt Mary's feelings on purpose. So rather than having a rant and calling the child names, you ask Mary, *"Hey, do you think Jonny was having a cactus day today?"* That simple question completely bypasses the child's usual response within themselves of *"Why did Jonny do that to me? What did I do wrong?"* It, very simply but effectively, transitions the child away from a negative self-narrative of *I must be the problem* to hey, *Jonny was just having an off day.* Now that is powerful. No self-judging or critical thinking, just *aaaggghhh was Jonny having a cactus day?* Let's remember to be kind towards Jonny. He's usually a flower friend and he normally has your back, so let's forgive him. Maybe he didn't sleep last night or maybe Mum understands that Jonny's mummy has a new baby in the house and they might all be lacking in sleep or Mum might know that Jonny's dad is away with work at the minute and he's probably really missing him. Just cut him some slack and be kind.

Kindness is free, effective, and very powerful. The beauty of this response is it removes any potential blame that your child might take responsibility for. It shifts from a reactive, potentially blaming thought process to a gentle, responsive, caring one. It is non-judgemental, loving kindness, and forgiveness going forward.

So what happens when you're growing up and a person moves into the realm of more cactus behaviour than flower behaviour? Again we are presented with a choice: as opposed to critical self-examination of what we could have possibly done wrong, I would ask Mary or Jonny how they feel in this person's company now. Do they feel safe in this person's company or are they on edge, fearful of a reaction to what they are about to say or do? Ask: *"Do they say bad things about you in front of your face?"* Your choice here is to decide how much time you are going to spend with this now-cactus person. If you don't feel good around them, then why are you spending time with them? There are choices to be made here, not judgements. If it's a fifty-fifty kinda thing, then your questions may center around being watchful of telling them personal stuff. It's not a bad thing to have lots of friends and only one or two close buddies who you share all your little treasures with.

How powerful is it for our children to learn at a young age that not everyone is for them and they are not for everyone either and that's okay? You get to choose who your friends are and it naturally evolves over time as we grow and mature. It's totally possible to navigate that journey in a way that is gentle and not emotionally painful.

I also at times apply the same cactus versus flower framework to my child. It's great because it allows you to have open conversations that are not as intense because of the language, but also because you are not ordering them around. Lots of people get to tell kiddies what to do all the time and they get rightly fed up with it. Especially for the anxious child…they spend too much time in their head on the best of days. For example, it's Friday night and your child has training but is feeling lethargic and wants to skip practice. Instead of getting into it and telling them they have to go, I'd say, *"Do you think you not turning up is cactus or flower behaviour towards your teammates and trainers? If you were giving of your free time to train kiddies, how would you receive somebody not bothering to show up? Think about those things before you make a decision, but also remember I think you should go and I think the idea of getting ready is putting you off, not the actual training because once you're there you spend half your time giggling. Also, your body enjoys movement, so are you being a cactus to your body too?"* If they choose not to attend, as much as that will frustrate me, I'll accept it, but also I will make it clear that they will have to apologise to their coach at the next session for their lack of attendance.

All the time I'm trying to honour their ability to make informed, measured choices and equally call it when they are trying to flake out. In general, having been given the time to process and weigh up all the pros and cons, they will make the right choice, building positive brain pathways that will serve them well into the future. They are looking inward when they are presented with choices, trusting their gut responses, and listening to their inner wisdom. Woo hoo, parenting win right there. Holy Grail achieved; that's our empowered, centred kiddies rocking their own wisdom!

## Chapter 7

# The Caring Habits and Deadly Habits

The Caring Habits and Deadly Habits are a list of behaviours which are listed below that I use to frame all the conversations that I have with my children and also my internal self-talk. I find that they help me cut to the heart of a matter and avoid mundane arguments about stuff. It provides a gentle but firm clear structure to base all conversations around. It can be particularly challenging to teach your children life lessons while also holding the energy of a supportive and nurturing parent. We have all, I believe, encountered the scenario of a child kicking off about wanting something or needing something to happen. When it's broken down and explored in a gentle but reflective way, we get to a place of learning what the need is behind the behaviour and exploring together if it can be achieved or not in any given moment. I believe our base instinct as a child is the need to be heard and listened to. The Caring Habits and Deadly Habits allow us as parents to provide this for our children in a way that's timely, effective, gentle, loving, and which aids our children taking ownership for how they feel.

**Seven Caring Habits**
1. Supporting
2. Encouraging
3. Listening
4. Accepting
5. Trusting
6. Respecting
7. Negotiating differences

**Seven Deadly Habits**
1. Criticizing
2. Blaming
3. Complaining
4. Nagging
5. Threatening
6. Punishing
7. Bribing, rewarding to control

Congratulations, you did it. Your family has managed to heal from the trauma of anxiety, and your child is shining, bright-eyed, full of joy and enthusiasm for life's experiences. They are naturally expressing their needs and feeling. That's kinda what the problem is though. They are totally rocking their new found confidence and expressive abilities and you can't shut them up. I'm not saying that you have created a monster, but it at times is challenging verbally.

Let's be honest, we don't always have the time or the will to constantly explore each other's needs. At times, we just need to get on with it. Oh Lord, is the cure worse than the disease. I can only speak for myself when I say that sometimes I find responding to my three kids exhausting. I fantasise about changing my name so I can stop hearing mommy every five seconds. Your dad is standing right beside you, so ask him a question! My brain struggles to think a thought to its natural conclusion because it's constantly getting interrupted. I now understand that I need quiet time and meditation time to balance that need in me.

Additionally, I also found that at times my now-empowered little human was very capable of pushing the boundaries and attempting to get their needs met promptly regardless of the impact on others. This wasn't the outcome I had dreamed of. I thought we'd be skipping through the meadow of flowers laughing and holding hands, not verbally wrestling for power. I don't want to argue with my children because it's exhausting, time-consuming, and it disconnects us. When parents and children have a verbal tennis match, the emotional temperature rises. Monkey brain in charge, defensive barriers go up, one winner one loser kind of scenario. It's not good for anyone.

Welcome to Choice Theory. William Glassier's theory is that nobody can 'make' us do or feel anything, as all we do is give or receive information. This information can neither make us do or feel anything. It is our choice how we perceive or filter the information, and it is our choice how we respond to it. It's a big step to accept, but if you can accept it, it will guide you and your family to a more responsible, empowered,relaxed, blame-free life. Let me use examples here to illustrate how I use it to empower my children's ability to take responsibility for their thoughts and reactions. And, more importantly, it teaches them how to set healthy boundaries and minimise the arguments in the house.

One of my children really struggled to get up in the morning. I was doing what millions of parents around the world do on school mornings: repeatedly calling one child to get up. I can't answer for you, but for me, I hate it. My emotional temperature soars pretty quickly. It's very frustrating first thing in the morning to see the other two kiddies up, dressed, bed made, and happily eating their breakfast. I am not one for comparing my children, and it's not a healthy habit. I read a quote years ago from Theodore Roosevelt that, "Comparison is the thief of joy" and I totally believe it to be true.

I called a family meeting, and I asked my child why he struggled to **_accept_** that he had to get up when called. I outlined to him that he was not **_listening_** or being **_respectful_** or **_accepting_** that he had to get up and give himself time for his breakfast. His response was, "*I don't mean to be. I just find it difficult to get up quickly.*"

"*Rubbish,*" I said. "*You hop out of the bed at the weekend to get to watch TV or play your Switch.*"

"*That's not true, Mam,*" he responded. "*At the weekend I get to lay there kinda daydreaming until I feel more awake. Then I get up.*"

Okay, my turn to demonstrate my caring habits abilities towards him. "*Okay, son, I'm listening. I hear your need to swim to the surface rather than be expected to jolt yourself into existence in the morning. How can we **negotiate the difference** here? I need you to get up without me calling you repeatedly and you need space and time to wake up.*" We agreed that I would call him, open his curtains, and allow him ten minutes to join the world. Once that ten minutes have passed, I'd call him again and, at that point, he gets up immediately. No faffing around.

It's working out perfectly, peace has been restored, both our needs meet, both parties listened to. The English dictionary definition of a compromise is "both parties reaching an agreement or settlement of a dispute by each side making a concession" or, as I regularly tell my kiddies, both sides feeling slightly dissatisfied. Has he tested the boundaries and not gotten up when I called him the second time? At the time of writing this, only once. Here's how I dealt with it. I advised him that he was now in danger of getting a consequence for not complying with an agreed norm in our family. I gave him an extra five minutes' grace just in case he was actually unwell, but my intuition felt he was just pushing his luck. Once the five minutes were up, I advised him that I was putting the timer on my watch and at this point he was choosing a consequence with his behaviour. I purposefully avoided getting into the deadly habits of *nagging* him to get up or *threatening* him if he didn't get up. Nope, my owl brain is more mature than yours and I'm driving here, not you, my then-seven-year-old.

He pushed it to the limit and only just chose to get ready in time, after a prompt from me reminding him that if he were not ready when I was leaving for school that his consequences would be severe. He had his breakfast in the car, and he went off to school. On his return, I provided him with the total amount of extra time he had chosen to spend in the bed. I explained that it was important to both his dad and I that he learn to make healthy choices for both himself and our little team. Therefore, we were giving him a consequence for each unhealthy choice he had taken. Were we being tough on him? Yes, for sure, but life can be tough and taking responsibility for your behaviour is vital for a happy existence, we believe. He did his own little chores that evening and his sisters'. He helped out whenever I did anything in the house, taking the washing out to the line or emptying the dishwasher. I'm mindful of giving rather than taking away anything. I'm also mindful of being close by so that when the child is ready to express what was going on or just ready to open up about the incident and discuss it, I'm available, all the time demonstrating that the problem occurred because of how they behaved, and that it was their behaviour and not them.

It took several evenings of extra chores to catch up on all the extra minutes he had chosen to spend in the bed. Once he was in a place of being open to discuss it, I firmly explained that his behaviour had a negative impact on me, his sisters, and the general energy of the house that morning. No one piece of our family puzzle is greater than the other. His needs are not going to be prioritized at the cost to anybody else, except in exceptional circumstances.

I don't think I know any woman that does not have a dieting story or hasn't at some stage in their existence restricted their eating or felt guilty for eating something bad, usually the bar of chocolate or the biscuits. My relationship with food is especially complex as, after years of resistance, I have accepted finally that my body cannot cope with wheat. I argued with myself in my head about this for years. I wanted to eat bread rolls and white toast and sticky buns. I deserved it. Gosh, the roller coaster of good days followed by bad days, the guilt the confusion, the *what's wrong with me?* inner dialogue. Then I started to apply the Caring Habits and Deadly Habits to the food choices I was making. Of course, I was free to eat all of the aforementioned but by eating them was I in the caring habits towards my body, if I felt ill after eating them why was I doing that to myself. Why was I struggling to accept that this wonderful powerful body I was blessed with did not function well when I consumed wheat. I was not listening to what it needed or communicating to me, I was blaming it for not being like everybody else's body. Comparison was stealing my joy! I feel I have a great relationship with myself now. I am in touch with how I want to feel and understand what to fuel my body with to support myself. Do I eat food that tastes great and is full of calories, yes, I totally enjoy them? I have invested time in listening to what my body wants to eat, what it enjoys, what fuels it with energy, vitality and keeps me healthy. I am now more mindful of my own needs so that my cup is full before I try to fill my children's cups.

# Chapter 8

# Additional Supports

## Sensory Needs

Sensory needs might be the best-kept secret from parents that I have ever encountered. In my envisioned dreamed of a child-centred, family-orientated, eco-friendly, needs-driven society, every child would automatically receive a sensory screen by an occupational therapist. Honestly, I am not equipped to explain to you the complexities of our sensory system and the extent of their impact on our children's behaviour. My very simplified explanation is that mainstream children can have sensory needs that can lead to challenging behaviour if not addressed. I am beyond grateful to Collette O'Hanlon (OT4KIDS) for allowing me to link both her inspired and detailed but simple and understandable explanation of sensory processing and her questionnaire with this book. Please refer to Appendix I for the "What is Sensory Integration?" and Appendix II the sensory screening questionnaire.

My advice is to approach this firstly from an open and observant perspective. Organise an evening with your parenting partner and fill out the sensory screener. Have a glass of wine, take your time with this, agree to hear each other, and negotiate any differences of opinion gently with each other. Remember, this is just an exploration of your child's behaviour patterns. It may lead to your child receiving some support if it's needed. Once completed, review the answers to see if a pattern has emerged. Focus in on the behaviours that have been highlighted and spend the coming week or ten days paying attention to when your child demonstrates them. Due to the fact that sensory needs are expressed through everyday behaviours, it's possible for us all to miss the signals. Once your allotted time of observation has expired, repeat the questionnaire and review answers. If one section is highlighted with yes, then this behaviour is frequent, and it indicates that perhaps your child requires support to integrate their sensory processing abilities in this area of their body.

## Craniosacral Therapy/Osteopath

I often thought about my child's arrival into this world. I wondered if her stressful, less than peaceful arrival had an impact on her personality. We know that children benefit in numerous ways from their journey down the birth canal, ranging from their microbiome to the alignment of their little bones. With this in mind, I consulted with a wonderful lady who is both an osteopath and craniosacral therapist. Like most of life's experiences, I did not appreciate the impact of this treatment until I experienced it myself. Wow, it has a powerful impact on the body. I would highly recommend taking your child. My family tends to go once a year, as it's possible for the body to require a re-adjustment due to stress or impact. In my dream of a holistic, prevention is better than cure world, every child would have a craniosacral treatment prior to leaving the hospital after delivery.

# Probiotics

Mental health and our body's health are one and the same thing. It's not possible to separate the two. If your child has struggled with chronic anxiety, it has impacted their gut health. Researchers at University College Cork have been studying the effects of probiotics on mental health. They report that when study participants take probiotics capsules for just one month, they experience less stress and anxiety and have lower levels of the stress hormone cortisol compared to the placebo group. Probiotics are naturally present in certain yoghurts, fermented milk, kefir, olives, and sauerkraut. Don't worry about trying to get these into your child's diet; supplement it to begin with. Do some research and find a brand that you are happy with. I give my children probiotics for two to three weeks at a time, usually when the seasons are changing. If you are interested in this topic, then I would recommend reading *Mad Diet* by Suzanne Lockhart and Dr. Patrick Holford's *The 10 Secrets of 100% Healthy People*.

# Tapping/Emotional Freedom Technique (EFT)

Emotional freedom technique is an alternative treatment for physical pain and emotional distress. It's also referred to as Tapping or psychological acupressure. People who use this technique believe tapping the body can create a balance in your energy system and treat pain. Though still being researched, EFT has been used to treat people with anxiety and post-traumatic stress disorder. It works by focusing on the meridian points or energy spots to restore balance to the body, thus releasing negative energy or emotions.

My child loves Brad Yates' tapping for sleep videos. Have a Google; there are hundreds available online dealing with sleep, anxiety, and much more. There are also many books on the subject, none of which I have had a chance to read yet. Gary Greg's *The EFT Manual* is a bestseller, as is Nick Ortner's *The Tapping Solution*.

## My Health Bible

Do you want to drive your own experience? Do you want to get the best out of each experience that life has for you? Do you want to give your body what it needs to shine? Then listen to your body. I totally believe that our bodies are in constant communication with us if we learn to listen. Disease can be perceived in a non-medical way. It can be perceived as *Dis-Ease* within the body. Similar to the approach used in tapping or acupuncture, there is the belief that a thought pattern and thus energy within the body can cause disease. We know that negative thought patterns produce uncomfortable and unrewarding experiences. Just like anxiety, learn to lean into it and consciously process what it's trying to communicate to you. Sounds overwhelming, but Louise Hay's Book *Heal your Body* will provide the link between what you're feeling and what it means for you. For example, in the book, it says that "anxiety's probable cause is the thought pattern of not trusting the flow and process of life." The new affirming thought patten or affirmation suggested is "I love and approve of myself; I trust the process of life. I am safe." It's, in my opinion, one of the most powerful books ever written and worth having.

## Food

If you can't pick it or kill it, don't eat it. If you can manage it, remove as much processed food as possible from your diet. I'm one for making life as easy to manage as possible, so my rule of thumb is how many ingredients are in this and can I understand what they are if I read them? If I need a science degree to understand what's in it, then it's not for me. How do I manage to do it all when food prep takes time? I batch cook, I freeze leftovers, and I couldn't live without my slow cooker. Food is medicine, and our anxious kiddies need lots of healthy nutrition to rebuild their bodies as they heal.

# Learning Style

*"Everybody is a genius. but if you judge a fish by its ability to climb a tree, it will live its whole life believing that it is stupid."*
**Albert Einstein**

I believe that we all bring something unique to the world. I am also mature enough to accept that, while I am far from silly, I am not gifted at learning certain subjects. I loved psychology in college until I had a lecturer who was into the statistics of psychological research, and then I struggled. Numbers are not my thing, but behaviour totally was. The only way I could remember anything from her lectures was to add a behaviour narrative to help me remember it. My brain likes stories but hates numbers. Can I please suggest that you do some research on learning styles to help your child understand their unique learning style from an early age? I believe it could be greatly beneficial both for their learning outcomes and confidence. It baffles me that all children are not routinely tested when they begin school as to what their learning style is. Imagine knowing how to fast track your learning abilities and present the information to yourself in a way that is more digestible for you.

## Homeopathy

I cannot recommend homeopathy enough. I am married to a PhD graduate scientist who works in the pharma medical arena. He is totally a show me the science, numbers, proof kind of person. He agreed, however, to turn to homeopathy when our child was struggling with a chronic condition that no amount of medical intervention was curing. She was coughing, lethargic, no appetite, and looked pale, and she had dull hair and eyes. She was losing her shine in front of my eyes and we had tried everything. Within one month of consulting with a homeopath, she returned to us. She has never had the cough since, she's bright, she eats like a horse, and her eyes are shining. Can I explain how it works? No. Can he? No. We have all been treated with homeopathy since then for both behavioural challenges and body ailments. Antionette McSweeney is my go-to for women's issues, and she also deals with children. Rita Cara Robinson and her team are also amazing. She and members of her team specialise in asthma, autism, and much more. They provide consults online and thus are available to anyone from all over the world.

## A Note on Words

Our words are enormously powerful and impactful. I am constantly telling my children that how you say something has a direct impact on how it's received. It's totally the same for how we speak to our children. Have you lay in your bed after a stressful day and thought that you were constantly giving out to your child that day? You feel the heavy energy of it and how it prevents loving connection between you, but you also struggle to know how to change. So, let's keep it simple and start with two simple ways to change how we talk to our kiddies.

Firstly, let's decide that from now on we will not use the word *don't*. I read somewhere that our brains do not recognise the word *don't*. This is especially true of teenagers. I chatted with a lady once in passing who was expressing her frustration that her child had left the milk out on the counter all day. She got home from work exasperated, thinking she had asked her child to do a simple thing. Don't leave the milk out! His brain only heard to leave the milk out. She said he looked completely perplexed, as he felt he had completed the requested task.

Naturally, when you consciously make the effort to not use *don't*, you are then aligned into a position of having to state what you require completed in the positive. Try it out now. Think of a chore or daily activity that you would like your child to achieve every day. For example, *"Don't forget to make your bed"* and then change it to *"Please remember to make your bed before you come down for breakfast."* Now say it aloud, and listen to the change in energy of how that would feel to be on the receiving end. Our children are constantly being told what to do. Adults in their lives, teachers, parents, coaches, and dance teachers. I believe in giving them choices and letting them live with the consequences of their choices, as was explored in the previous chapter.

If you're brave enough, pop on your big girl pants here and ask yourself, "Am I holding myself to the same standard that I am expecting from my child?"

## Parental Self-Care

Take some time out. It can be incredibly challenging for the parent of an anxious child to catch some downtime. Meeting the anxious child's need for constant reassurance or their emotional outbursts is exhausting. Get away, and I mean really away. Once I had achieved the point with my child where she had the ability to sleep restfully, I took a few days away on my own. I said I was working on this book, which I was, but not direct work. I was restoring my own self. This book was not going to be birthed by the exhausted mommy I was then. I went far enough away that I could not come home on a guilt whim. I actually did bring my computer and achieved some work, but not before I had walked, watched daytime T.V., explored the local town of beautiful Clifden. I had a coffee at a café and people watched. I sat by the river and just listened to nature. I restored my soul. We cannot give from an empty cup. Learn to fill your own first. In my experience, the mommy is the emotional glue that holds a family together. We must learn to meet our own needs if we want to meet the needs of our loved ones.

I really struggled with leaving my children. It was very difficult for me. I felt guilty. So, I decided I needed to reframe the leaving into "I'm teaching them." Children learn a lot through watching us. They watch how we respond and interact and how we meet our own needs. I started to ask myself, "How would I like my children to behave when they are adults and parents?" I'd want them to have a career, go to an exercise class, have adult nights out, and retain a piece of themselves outside of meeting their family's needs. It was a gamechanger for me. If they see me meeting my needs in balance with theirs, then they are more likely to do it for themselves. I hope this inspires you in some way to carve out time for yourself. If you're happy, they are more likely to be happy.

This list is by no means exhaustive. Do what feels right for you and resonates for you intuitively. I have not discussed reflexology, message, acupuncture, energy healing in all its forms such as Rahanni or Reiki, pedicures, or manicures. Do what sparks joy for you and you won't go too far wrong.

## The Wishing Tree

Essentially everything on this earth was first created in the mind. Wonderful things and horrible things started off life in somebody's mind. In the Yogic tradition, a well-organised mind is referred to as a Wishing Tree. The belief is that if you manage to organise your thinking, it in turn organises your whole system; your body, emotions and energies get aligned to your highest good. You get in touch with your inner light, your creativity. Essentially you become a Wishing Tree. Anything you wish for will happen.

There is a beautiful story in the Yogic lore. A man went for a walk and accidentally walked into paradise. After a long walk, he felt a little tired and thought, "*I wish I could rest somewhere.*" He spotted a beautiful tree with soft grass underneath. He lay down and enjoyed a restful sleep. He woke up rested and thought, "*I am hungry. I wish I had something to eat.*" He thought of all the nice things he'd like to eat and all of them just appeared before him. He enjoyed the food and then thought, "*I am thirsty.*" Again, he wished for something to drink. Instantly, drinks appeared before him.

An unorganised mind is referred to as the monkey mind in Yogic Lore. When the man's monkey mind became active, he thought, "*What the hell is happening here?*" I ask and instantly receive, "*Maybe there are ghosts around?*" He looked and there were ghosts present. "*Maybe they will torture me?*" And they did torture him. He thought, "*Oh, they are going to kill me*" and they did indeed kill him.

The problem was he was sitting under a Wishing Tree. Whatever he wished for became a reality. You need to develop your mind to a point where it becomes a wishing tree, not a playground for the monkey to torture you with thoughts of what you are scared of.

Yogic lore believes that all humans strive to live joyfully and peacefully. In terms of relationships, we want them to be loving and affectionate. All human beings want peaceful relationships within themselves and in their environment. If it happens in our bodies, we call it health, and when it happens in our mind, we call it peace and joy. In our emotions, we call it love and compassion, and in our energy, we call it bliss and ecstasy. No matter what your job or your status as a human, we are all looking for the same thing: happy, loving connections.

If you can learn to organise your monkey brain and align your mind, body, emotions, and energy in one direction, you can become creative. What you want to create will happen effortlessly. Once you are organised, you become your own Wishing Tree, and you now have the power to let your creativity shine.

*Effectively living your Wisdom's Wishes.*

# Acknowledgements

*"Everything you have now was once only imagined."*
**Wayne Dyer**

This book exists because of other people. A complete list of influencers is not practical or achievable. Forgive me if I have not mentioned you.

To my Mum and Dad, you gifted me with a love and appreciation for community and Mother Nature's cycles.

To my extended family, thanks for putting up with me. It is not an easy task.

To my friends, especially Joanne and Gemma, I feel blessed to have you in my life.

To Marineta Viegas the creative genius behind Relax Kids. Thank you seems so small considering the impact your programme has had on my life, my family, and countless others. I hope this book helps spread the love.

To all the children who have ever attended my Relax Kids classes, thank you for teaching me.

To the families that trust me with their most prized gift, their children, thank you for allowing me to be part of your journey and sharing your truth with me. There is a little lesson from you all on these pages, and this book is better because of your input.

To my husband, you are my rock. You challenge me, drive me nuts, and remind me constantly that I have a unique perspective to share with the world. Without your love support and a firm push regularly, I would not have completed this book.

To my children, my greatest challenge, my greatest teachers. I have been blessed with an encyclopedia/comedian, sport fanatic/engineer plus a creative/expressive. I am so lucky you choose me to be your mum. Love you all to the moon and back.

To you the reader, thank you for purchasing my book. I hope you found what you were seeking within its pages. I hope it changed your perception of yourself and your abilities. Marianne Williamson, in her book *A Return to Love*, writes that "A miracle is just a shift in perception."

I choose to believe in miracles; I see them often. I hope you will too.

### *Bonus*

Please do connect with me via the private Facebook group linked below:

https://www.facebook.com/groups/wisdomswishes

# Please Review

Thank you for reading this book.

If you found this book helpful, please help me spread the message to parents and caregivers around the world.

Please visit Amazon, or the platform where you purchased this book, or Goodreads, to write a review. This matters because most potential readers first judge a book by what others have to say.

Thank you

Sinéad

## Recommended Reading List

- **The Dream Machine** by Relax Kids
  Unlock your child's imagination just before bedtime. This book cleverly allows the reader to participate and choose their destination each evening.

- **A Monster Handbook** by relax kids
  A toolkit of strategies and exercises to help your child manage big feelings. It's a book we use regularly.

- **The Wishing Star** by Relax Kids
  Meditations for children to use at any time to restore calm. My firm favorite is The Magic Tree. The closing statement is "Everything I need is inside me".

- **E Squared** by Pam Grout
  It's a list of experiments that you carry out to test the theory that "what you think about you bring about."

- **The Universe Has Your Back** by Gabby Bernstein
  Brilliant book to guide your thinking process and unpack some of our learned behaviors. Great book to help move away from fearful thinking.

- **Heal Your Body** by Louise Hay
  Do you have a recurring health issue? This book outlines the mental causes for physical illnesses.

- **Your Fantastic Elastic Brain** by Joann Deak
  Brilliant for children to learn about how their brain works for ages 6 upwards.

- **The Indigo Children** by Lee Carroll and Jan Tober
  This one is for you if your child is always switched on emotionally and mentally. If you have a sense that your child is very smart and has deep insight, then this one's for you.

- **Ten Mindful Minutes** by Goldie Hawn
  Great practical advice on how to respond to your children mindfully, helping you move away from reactive action to more thoughtful responses to their needs behind behavior.

- **The Explosive Child** by Ross W Green.
  If you're frustrated, angry, overwhelmed, and feel you are not equipped to meet your child's needs, this book will help you understand why and how to respond in a way that is nonpunitive, humane, and effective.

- **Cotton Wool Kids** by Sheila O'Malley
  Are you obsessed with safety, progress, and development? Constantly afraid of predators, or keeping your children over-supervised? This book gives parents strategies to handle the pressure of society and media and encourages them to raise their children with a more relaxed and joyful approach.

- **The Whole Brain Child** and **The Yes Brain Child** by Daniel J. Siegel & Tina Payne Bryson
  Parenting to promote brain development, leading to calmer, happier children. Using their twelve strategies, you can turn outbursts, arguments, or fear into a chance to integrate your child's brain and foster vital growth.

- **RELAX KIDS**

  There is a vast array of resources available, both free and to purchase, on the Relax Kids website. Monthly affirmation calendars and a twenty-one-day family pack which you can download for free. This includes MP3 tracks to play at nighttime.

- I also love the free App **Insight Timer** for meditations.

# Appendix I
# What is Sensory Integration?

Sensory integration/sensory processing is the process by which our brains receive information through our senses and organise this information, so that we can do the things that we need to do in our everyday lives. For example, our children need to be regulated so that they can play, focus, and learn every day.

We have eight senses in total. Most of us are familiar with five of these—sight, hearing, taste, smell, and touch—the other three senses tend to be less well-known. These are:

1.  *Proprioception* (ability to know where our bodies are positioned/body awareness).

2.  *Vestibular* (awareness of balance and movement).

3.  *Interoception* (a fairly newly researched sense which is how our bodies tell our brain what is going on inside our body, for example, if we are hungry, if our hearts are beating very fast, if we have butterflies in our stomachs, etc.).

Sensory integration is also the term used to describe the intervention/treatment of a sensory processing difficulty.

We all have our own individual sensory preferences: some of us love massages, wearing woolly jumpers, or walking barefoot, while others could think of nothing worse! Some of us love the smell of fresh-cut grass, while others close the window. Sensory preferences are fine; they make us who we are. Sensory issues, however, can develop when we are unable to complete activities that we need to because we are unable to tolerate the type of sensory input associated with them. Do any of these traits sound familiar?

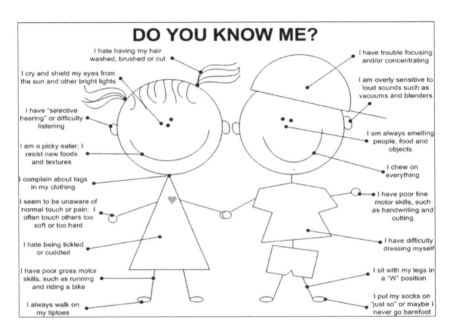

These children have sensory processing issues. Not all children with sensory processing difficulties will have all of these issues, *but a cluster of these would indicate that an Occupational Therapy Sensory Assessment may be beneficial.*

We all have our own unique way in which we modulate or control the sensory input we receive. A person who is able to modulate well notices the sensory input they are receiving as soon as it comes into their sensory system and filters out the unimportant information, so that emotions and behaviour reflect appropriate responses to the situation or environment. Research would support the idea that while one does not cause the other, sensory processing and behavioural issues often co-exist, with behaviours becoming more apparent and overt when the child is dysregulated and less able to control their responses to sensory input. When this happens to be the case, ***taking small measures to meet your child's sensory needs*** will have a ***huge impact*** on their day-to-day experiences at home, at school, and at out-of-school activities.

If children's sensory needs are being met on a *regular* basis, before they reach the point where they need to "sensory seek," then any undesirable sensory-seeking types of behavior will usually desist.

Some children have difficulty interpreting the sensory input they receive, and they can be ***under-responsive and over-responsive*** to different types of input.

Children with **sensory over-responsivity** (sometimes called "sensory defensiveness") respond to sensory messages **more intensely, more quickly, and/or for a longer time** than children with normal sensory responsivity." *Miller, LJ (2006) Sensational Kids: Hope and Help for Children with Sensory Processing Disorder (SPD)

This means that a sensation may be perceived as **"painful"** and the child may have a **"fright, flight, fight"** response. Children who are **"under-responsive"** to sensory information in the classroom may generally **be viewed as lazy, unmotivated, stubborn, or defiant**. These children typically need sensory stimulation that is stronger, lasts longer, and is more frequent than that of their peers.

Children can have a **combination of responses** to different types of sensory input, and their responses can change depending on the time of day, how many other sensory experiences they have had on any given day, etc.

A child who is a ***SENSORY AVOIDER*** can get quickly overstimulated, and in order to stop reaching this point of overload the sensory avoiding child will take action, e.g., they may remove themselves from the situation by running, hiding, or perhaps having a tantrum to avoid being taken somewhere that is **intolerable for them from a sensory perspective**. This child may also seem quiet, withdrawn, and lacking in attention; however, they are likely to be keeping an eye out for potential situations/things which may cause overstimulation. These **children may appear to lack concentration/attention** because their main point of focus is on identifying potentially distressing sensory experiences and attempting to avoid them. This child can also **appear fearful and uncooperative**, when in fact they are attempting to preserve/save themselves from potentially upsetting sensory experiences. This child will benefit from routine, predictability, and calming, proprioceptive experiences, which will allow them to become **more confident** in their environment and also help them **to regulate their Central Nervous System so that they can cope better with new/challenging sensory input**.

The child who is a **SENSORY SEEKER** appears to be in constant motion and is always on the move. This child can have **difficulty paying attention** and may often **appear impulsive** in their actions. The sensory-seeking child is usually moving because he/she is trying to get the sensory input that their system needs to stay focused and on task, but with too much or inappropriate input, this child **can quickly become dysregulated and overstimulated**. This child can appear uncoordinated and clumsy and often takes lots of risks in their play. These children need a sensory programme providing regular, intense proprioceptive input to "feed" their sensory system, providing the sensory system with the input it needs to achieve and maintain a state of calm and regulation and avoid reaching a state of overstimulation.

The child who is **SENSORY SENSITIVE** is said to have a **low threshold for sensory input**, which means it does not take much input to switch the child into a state of **over-arousal/dysregulation**. This child can have **difficulty paying attention and staying focused** and can be very easily distracted by any sensory input, e.g., noise, smell, touch, movement, etc. This child can appear to respond negatively to situations and often his/her responses can seem out of proportion to the input received or the situation. This child is likely to benefit from regular, calming proprioceptive input and a "chill out" or "safe space" to retreat to when they are overstimulated.

The child who has **LOW REGISTRATION OF SENSORY INPUT** can appear to let the world pass them by and may often be described as **lazy or lethargic.** These children need a wider variety and more intense input to activate their system and help them to achieve what is often referred to as the "just right state" of arousal, which is essential for focus and learning. Without intense and regular input, these children often appear disinterested and lacking in focus.

**What behaviours would you expect to see in a sensory defensive child?**

Primary defensive behaviours include negative, avoidant, aversive, or defensive reactions to sensory experiences. As a result of sensory defensiveness, children can appear stressed, anxious, or distractible.

A sensory defensive child can present with a lot of controlling or even obsessive behaviours.

- They may have difficulty sleeping.

- Difficulties such as social avoidance, fighting, or aggressive behaviours, emotional fragility, or 'meltdowns' are common because social and emotional disruptions result in patterns of learned behaviours, habits, and interaction styles that are protective and defensive in nature.

Children may use coping strategies to help manage sensory defensiveness. Common coping strategies include:

Avoidance of the sensations, events, environments, or social interactions.

Controlling or obsessive behaviours such as rigid routines or producing loud sounds to block auditory irritations.

Cognitive strategies such as self-talk and enduring aversive sensations for a short time.

Sensory-seeking behaviours include repetitive actions, craving pressure, heavy muscle action, mouthing, sucking, biting objects, jaw clenching.

**Managing Sensory Sensitivities**

Here are some general ideas that may be helpful. Please note that these are generic in nature and may not completely address your child's sensory needs. An Occupational Therapy Assessment and provision of an individual Sensory Diet would be able to help determine your child's exact and individual needs; however, some of these ideas may prove useful.

- Routine can be a lifesaver! Keeping the same order of activities as much as possible during the day can help.

- Give your child lots of notice if there is going to be a change in routine, especially one which can be overwhelming (someone coming to visit, an outing, leaving home early).

- Avoid doing "too much" in a day (shopping, then a party. then visit to the park). You are likely to overstimulate a child who may already be sensory sensitive child.

The following "universal modulators" may be useful:

- Movement – Slow and controlled rocking, swaying, and rhythmical movement can be calming.

- Deep pressure – Massage, bear hugs, etc.

- Proprioception – Jumping, stretching, taking weight through your arms.

- Heavy work – Pushing, pulling, climbing, running, carrying (this usually combines movement, deep pressure, and proprioception). Be sure that this is in a controlled way and not random, jerky, fast way, as this type of input may actually overstimulate a child.

- Seclusion – Try to identify a safe space where the child can go if they are feeling overwhelmed. It is important that this is a comfortable place and that it is not used as a punishment. Try a small pop-up tent in the corner of a bedroom. This will help reduce environmental distractions. Encourage your child to pick some items that they find calming that they can keep in here, such as fidgets or a beanbag to lie on.

- Try to provide/encourage calming input **_before_** the child reaches a state of sensory overload, as these strategies will not work if the child is already in a sensory overload/meltdown.

If you feel your child may have issues with sensory processing input and the strategies above are not quite meeting their needs, you may need to contact an Occupational Therapist for an assessment of your child's sensory processing.

Please feel free to contact, Colette O'Hanlon, Senior Occupational Therapist, with any queries.

Phone:+ 353 85 749 2732

Email: ot4kidscoh@gmail.com

# Appendix II
# Occupational Therapy Sensory Screening Tool

### Occupational Therapy Sensory Screening Tool

Name _____ DOB_____ Age_____

Form Completed by_____Relationship to child _____

Date Form Completed by_____

Please put an X in the column which applies best to your child:

| Touch/Tactile | Present Most of Time | Absent Most of Time |
|---|---|---|
| Gets stressed by seams in socks | | |
| Gets distressed by tags on clothes | | |
| Is bothered by rough bed sheets | | |
| Is bothered by rough textured clothing eg denim | | |
| Gets distressed having face washed | | |
| Gets distressed having nails cut | | |
| Gets distressed having hair cut | | |
| Gets distressed in bath | | |
| Get distressed in shower | | |
| Dislikes hair washing | | |
| Dislikes hair brushing | | |
| Avoids/Dislikes messy play eg sand, water, paint | | |
| Prefers to be naked | | |
| Mouths objects constantly | | |
| Thoroughly enjoys and seeks out messy play | | |
| Craves vibrating or strong sensory input | | |
| Craves touch – especially deep pressure | | |
| Is not aware of being touched | | |
| May not be aware that hands/face are dirty or feel his/her nose running | | |
| Repeatedly touches objects or surfaces that are soothing (eg blanket) | | |
| Seeks out surfaces that provide strong tactile feedback (eg. Extremely rough/bumpy surfaces or extremely smooth/soft surfaces) | | |
| Has a preference and craving for excessively spicy, sweet, sour or salty foods | | |
| Has difficulty with fine motor tasks such as zipping/buttoning clothes, using scissors, crayons or cutlery | | |
| Will turn head to look at a part of their body when it is touched | | |

| | | |
|---|---|---|
| Not able to identify objects by touch alone | | |
| Is easily upset by minor injuries (eg bumps, scrapes) | | |
| Withdraws from splashing water | | |
| Rubs or scratches a spot that has been touched | | |

| Movement | Present Most of Time | Absent Most of Time |
|---|---|---|
| Looses balance easily and may appear clumsy | | |
| Fearful of feet leaving the ground | | |
| Afraid of heights, even the height of a step or kerb | | |
| Avoids rapid or rotating/spinning movements eg spinning | | |
| Avoids/Dislikes playground activities eg swings and slides | | |
| Prefers sedentary tasks, moves slowly and cautiously and avoids taking risks | | |
| Terrified of falling even when there is no risk of it | | |
| Fearful of going up or down stairs or walking on uneven surfaces | | |
| Afraid of being tipped upside down, sideways or backwards | | |
| Is fidgety/seeks all kinds of movement and this interferes with daily routines | | |
| Dislikes riding in a moving car | | |
| Twirls/spins self throughout the day | | |
| Rocks: whole body side to side | | |
| Rocks: whole body back and forth | | |
| Bangs head against firm surfaces | | |
| Loves being tossed in the air | | |
| Always jumping on furniture, trampolines | | |
| Has a limp "floppy" body | | |
| Often sits in "W" position | | |
| Fatigues easily | | |
| Has difficulty licking an ice cream cone | | |

| | Present Most of Time | Absent Most of Time |
|---|---|---|
| Difficulty learning dance or exercise sequences | | |
| Poor Body awareness: bumps into things, knocks things over, trips appears clumsy | | |
| Frequently slumps, lies down and/or leans head on hand while working at his/her desk | | |
| Poor gross motor skills, jumping, catching a ball, running etc | | |

| Proprioception | Present Most of Time | Absent Most of Time |
|---|---|---|
| Stamps feet when walking | | |
| Seeks out crashing, jumping, banging activities | | |
| Frequently falls on the floor intentionally | | |
| Loves banging/pushing/pulling objects | | |
| Excessive banging on/with toys or other objects | | |
| Loves jumping off furniture or from high places | | |
| Loves wrestling or other tackling games | | |
| Kicks his/her feet on floor/chair while sitting at desk | | |
| Bites or sucks on fingers | | |
| Cracks his/her knuckles | | |
| Loves to be tightly wrapped in many or weighted blankets, especially at bedtime | | |
| Prefers clothes to be as tight as possible | | |
| Difficulty when drawing or colouring may be too light to see or so hard the tip of the pencil breaks | | |
| Misjudges the weight of an object for example picks up a glass of water with such force that it spills or complains that it is too heavy | | |

| Auditory Stimulation | Present Most of Time | Absent Most of Time |
|---|---|---|
| Distracted by sounds not normally noticed by others eg humming of fridge, fans or clocks ticking | | |
| Fearful of the sound of a flushing toilet, vacuum, hairdryer, squeaky shoes etc | | |
| Decides whether they like people based on the sound of their voice | | |
| Loves excessively loud music or television | | |
| Appears oblivious to certain sounds | | |
| Talks self through a task, often out loud | | |
| Often does not respond to verbal cues or to name being called | | |

| | | |
|---|---|---|
| Appears confused about where a sound is coming from | | |
| Holds hands over ears to protect ears from sound | | |
| Enjoys strange noises/makes noises for noise's sake | | |
| Becomes distressed during assemblies or gatherings of people | | |

| Olfactory Stimulation | Present Most of Time | Absent Most of Time |
|---|---|---|
| Bothered by household cooking smells | | |
| Use smell to interact with others | | |
| Notices or is bothered by smells that others donot notice | | |

| Visual Stimulation | Present Most of Time | Absent Most of Time |
|---|---|---|
| Enjoys playing in the dark | | |
| Becomes distressed in dark or dimly lit rooms | | |
| Sensitive to bright lights; will squint, cover eyes, cry | | |
| Easily distracted by visual stimuli around the room; movement, lights, windows, lights | | |
| Avoids eye contact | | |
| Flicks objects near or in front of his/her eyes | | |

| Oral Sensory Processing | Not At All | Sometimes | Always |
|---|---|---|---|
| Eats a variety of foods | | | |
| Drinks a wide range of liquids | | | |
| Gags, vomits or coughs easily with food textures or utensils in mouth | | | |
| Spits out his/her food when eating | | | |
| Becomes upset when food is placed in front of him at mealtimes | | | |
| Refuses to eat food in the presence of others | | | |
| Appears to have weak muscles affecting posture for sitting (e.g. slumps at the table) | | | |
| Eats independently | | | |
| Uses fingers to eat | | | |
| Uses cutlery for eating: (Please circle) fork    knife    spoon | | | |
| Drinks from: (Please circle) Bottle    Sippy Cup/Beaker    Sports Bottle    Straw    Cup | | | |
| Swallows without first chewing food | | | |
| Seems to struggle with foods e.g. meats which require lots of chewing | | | |
| Drinks without spilling | | | |

| | | | |
|---|---|---|---|
| Drools | | | |
| Stuffs his/her mouth with food | | | |
| Takes tiny, mouse size bites | | | |
| Uses drinks to wash down bites of food | | | |
| Avoids certain tastes that are typically part of children's diets | | | |
| Avoids certain smells that are typically part of children's diets | | | |
| Routinely smells non-food objects | | | |
| Shows strong preference for certain tastes. List:<br>•<br>•<br>•<br>• | | | |
| Chews or licks non-food objects | | | |
| Mouths objects (for example pencil, hands) | | | |
| Bites others or himself | | | |
| Dislikes handling food | | | |
| Dislikes different foods touching one another on the plate | | | |
| Seeks out vibration to the mouth area e.g. vibrating pens, mouth toys, toothbrush | | | |
| Rubs, squeezes or pushes hands into the chin area | | | |

Please complete the following table with regard to food texture and temperature:

| Type of food/ drink | List foods | Not At All | Sometimes | Always |
|---|---|---|---|---|
| Drinks | | | | |
| Pureed foods e.g. pudding, applesauce, blended meats/ vegetables | | | | |
| Soft or mushy/mashed foods e.g. jelly, peas, mashed potato, bananas / eggs | | | | |
| Ground foods e.g. crumbled meats, scrambled eggs, cottage cheese, small pieces of toast, crackers | | | | |
| Chopped foods e.g. fruit salad, chopped carrot | | | | |
| Whole foods e.g. bananas, potatoes, large pieces of meat such as chicken nuggets | | | | |
| Chewy e.g. wine gums, chewing gum, meat, bagels, jam-centred biscuits, bars | | | | |
| Type of food/ drink | List foods | Not At All | Sometimes | Always |
| Crunchy e.g. apples, cereal, crisps, raw vegetables, biscuits | | | | |
| Cold Foods e.g. ice cream, yoghurt, eating hot meals cold | | | | |

Signed:............................................................ Date:...............................

# Please Review

Dear Reader,

If you enjoyed this book, would you kindly post a short review on Amazon? Your feedback will make all the difference to getting the word out about this book.

To leave a review, go to Amazon and type in the book title. When you have found it and go to the book page, please scroll to the bottom of the page to where it says 'Write a Review' and then submit your review.

Thank you in advance.

Sinéad

# Next Steps

I'm delighted you have read this book, now do something. Take an action step. Choose something that resonates with you and do it, make the appointment. There is no escalator to health and wellness you have to take the stairs or as my mammy would always say "move yourself".

If you feel I am the right fit, then please choose one of the following options:

Connect in with the private Facebook group for support and connection with other parents and myself. My vision is that the group will evolve over time and it's direction will be driven by the needs expressed by its members.

https://www.facebook.com/groups/wisdomswishes

If you feel your family would benefit from a Family Anxiety session, then please book an Initial Consultation call with me to explore if I am the right solution for your family's needs. The no obligation call can be booked through my website.

https://www.sineadflanagan.ie/familyanxietysessions

Are you a School Principal looking to support the wellbeing of your pupils and staff? I offer classes, teacher wellness sessions, anxiety workshops for pupils and parents. I can also work with you on a bespoke offering for your school. Please see link below for further details.

https://www.sineadflanagan.ie/relaxkids

https://www.sineadflanagan.ie/teachersupport

If you would like to stay connected with me, please avail of one of the following options:

https://www.facebook.com/RelaxKidsSinead

https://www.instagram.com/flanaganSinead273/

www.linkedin.com/in/Sineadflanagan

Alternatively, you can email me on_hello@sineadflanagan.ie